PRINCEWILL LAGANG

E-commerce Evolution: Building a 21st Century Brand

Contents

1

E-commerce Evolution: Building a 21st Century Brand

The Birth of E-commerce

In the not-so-distant past, the concept of buying products and services from the comfort of one's own home was nothing more than a fantasy. Today, it's a daily reality for millions of people around the world. The rapid evolution of e-commerce has transformed the way we shop, interact with brands, and conduct business. This chapter marks the beginning of our journey into the fascinating world of e-commerce and brand-building in the 21st century.

The Early Days of E-commerce

E-commerce, short for electronic commerce, can be traced back to the 11070s when early experiments with online transactions began. However, it wasn't until the mid-110100s that e-commerce truly began to take shape, thanks to pioneers like Amazon and eBay. These platforms laid the groundwork for the digital shopping experience we know today. In the late 110100s and early

2000s, the dot-com bubble burst, and many e-commerce startups collapsed. This period of turbulence marked an important lesson – the importance of sound business fundamentals, even in the digital world.

The E-commerce Revolution

As the internet became more accessible, e-commerce saw exponential growth. Traditional brick-and-mortar businesses adapted to this new landscape, and new, innovative digital-native brands emerged. People started to trust online transactions, and security measures improved. The convenience of shopping online, along with the ability to compare products, read reviews, and receive personalized recommendations, fueled the e-commerce revolution.

Building a 21st Century Brand

In the 21st century, a brand isn't just a logo and a name; it's an experience. E-commerce has not only changed the way we shop but has also redefined how brands connect with their customers. Building a brand in this era involves a complex mix of technology, data, marketing, and customer-centricity. Brands need to resonate with the values and aspirations of their target audience, providing an emotional connection that goes beyond the product itself.

The Digital Consumer

Understanding the digital consumer is fundamental to building a successful 21st-century brand. Today's consumers are savvy, well-informed, and highly selective. They demand more than just a product; they seek value, authenticity, and a seamless shopping experience. As an e-commerce brand, your ability to meet and exceed these expectations will determine your success.

The E-commerce Ecosystem

To navigate the e-commerce landscape effectively, you need to understand the ecosystem. This includes not only your online store but also various channels, such as social media, marketplaces, and advertising platforms. You'll learn to harness the power of data and analytics to drive growth, and to adapt to the ever-evolving world of technology and consumer behavior.

What to Expect in This Book

In the chapters that follow, we'll delve deep into the intricacies of e-commerce and brand-building in the 21st century. You'll explore strategies for product development, digital marketing, customer engagement, and the management of an e-commerce business. You'll gain insights into the role of technology, the importance of sustainability, and the impact of global trends on e-commerce.

The journey begins here, and I invite you to embark on this exciting exploration of e-commerce's evolution and the art of building a 21st-century brand. By the end of this book, you'll be equipped with the knowledge and tools to thrive in the ever-changing landscape of e-commerce and create a brand that leaves a lasting mark in the digital age.

In the coming chapters, we'll dive deeper into the strategies, challenges, and opportunities that lie ahead. So, fasten your seatbelts and get ready to transform your e-commerce venture into a 21st-century brand that stands the test of time.

2

The Foundations of E-commerce

Building Blocks for E-commerce Success

In the previous chapter, we explored the evolution of e-commerce and the changing landscape of brand-building in the 21st century. Now, let's delve deeper into the foundations of e-commerce and discover the essential building blocks for success in this digital age.

The E-commerce Business Model

At the heart of every successful e-commerce venture is a well-defined business model. Whether you're selling physical products, digital goods, services, or a combination of these, your business model should align with your target market and your unique value proposition. In this chapter, we'll examine various e-commerce business models, from dropshipping and subscription services to traditional online retail, and help you choose the one that best suits your goals.

Choosing Your Niche

E-commerce success often hinges on the ability to identify and dominate a niche market. The days of one-size-fits-all retail are long gone. By understanding your target audience's needs, preferences, and pain points, you can create a brand that speaks directly to them. We'll explore the importance of market research, competitive analysis, and trend spotting to select the perfect niche for your e-commerce business.

Product Sourcing and Quality

The products you offer play a pivotal role in your e-commerce brand's success. Whether you're manufacturing your own products or sourcing from suppliers, quality and consistency are non-negotiable. We'll discuss the nuances of product sourcing, including overseas suppliers, local artisans, and ethical considerations. You'll learn how to ensure your products meet the highest standards to build trust with your customers.

E-commerce Technology Stack

To run a successful online store, you need a robust technology stack. We'll dissect the components of this stack, from e-commerce platforms and content management systems to payment gateways and customer relationship management (CRM) systems. You'll gain insights into selecting the right tools and technologies that align with your business model and goals.

Website Design and User Experience

Your e-commerce website is your storefront in the digital world, and it needs to leave a lasting impression. In this chapter, we'll discuss the principles of effective web design and user experience (UX) to ensure your visitors have a seamless and enjoyable shopping journey. We'll explore responsive design, mobile optimization, and the use of persuasive design elements to boost conversion rates.

Building Trust and Credibility

Trust is the currency of e-commerce. Customers need to trust your brand before they make a purchase. We'll explore strategies for building trust, including transparent pricing, customer reviews, security measures, and a strong online presence. Trust not only leads to conversions but also fosters customer loyalty.

Setting Up Shop: Legal and Regulatory Considerations

The e-commerce landscape is subject to a complex web of legal and regulatory requirements. From intellectual property rights to data privacy and international trade regulations, we'll guide you through the essential legal considerations to protect your business and avoid costly pitfalls.

Financial Management

Effective financial management is critical to the sustainability and growth of your e-commerce business. In this chapter, we'll discuss topics such as pricing strategies, inventory management, and financial forecasting. You'll learn how to keep your financial house in order and make informed decisions for your business's future.

Key Takeaways

In this chapter, we've laid the groundwork for your e-commerce journey by exploring the fundamental components of a successful e-commerce business. These building blocks will serve as the foundation for your brand's growth and evolution. As you move forward, you'll be better equipped to make informed decisions and navigate the complexities of the e-commerce world.

In Chapter 3, we'll shift our focus to the core strategies for product development and selection. We'll delve into how to create, curate, and present products that resonate with your target audience, align with your brand's values, and set you on the path to e-commerce success.

—-

This chapter provides readers with the essential foundations of e-commerce, helping them understand the critical elements necessary for building a successful online business. Subsequent chapters can then explore each of these foundational topics in greater detail, offering practical guidance and insights to assist your readers in their e-commerce journey.

3

Crafting Compelling Products for Your E-commerce Brand

Mastering the Art of Product Development and Selection

In the previous chapters, we established the foundation for your e-commerce business. Now, it's time to dive into the heart of your brand: your products. Chapter 3 explores the art and science of crafting and selecting products that will not only meet your customers' needs but also set your brand apart in the competitive e-commerce landscape.

Understanding Your Target Audience

Before you can begin developing or curating products, you must intimately understand your target audience. In this chapter, we'll explore the techniques and tools to create detailed customer personas. These profiles will help you identify your customers' preferences, pain points, and aspirations, allowing you to tailor your product offerings to their specific needs.

Product Development: From Idea to Reality

If you plan to create your own products, this section will guide you through the product development process. We'll discuss brainstorming and idea generation, prototyping, testing, and the intricacies of design, manufacturing, and quality control. You'll learn how to turn a concept into a tangible product that resonates with your audience.

Curating Products: Selecting the Right Mix

For those focusing on product curation or dropshipping, this chapter explores the art of selecting products that align with your brand's vision. We'll discuss the importance of product-market fit, competitive analysis, and the criteria to consider when evaluating potential products for your e-commerce store. You'll gain insights into sourcing, pricing, and inventory management.

Sustainability and Ethical Considerations

In the 21st century, consumers are increasingly conscious of the environmental and ethical impact of their purchases. This section delves into the importance of sustainability and ethics in product selection. We'll explore eco-friendly sourcing, fair trade practices, and the role of corporate social responsibility in building a brand with purpose.

Product Presentation and Storytelling

Your product's presentation can make or break a sale. We'll examine the art of product photography, detailed product descriptions, and the use of storytelling to engage and captivate your audience. A compelling product story can turn an ordinary item into an aspirational purchase.

Personalization and Customization

In a world of mass-produced goods, offering personalization and customization options can set your brand apart. We'll explore the benefits and challenges of tailoring products to individual customer preferences and how it can drive customer loyalty and higher margins.

Testing and Iteration

Once your products are in the market, the journey doesn't end. We'll discuss the importance of ongoing testing and iteration. You'll learn how to gather and analyze customer feedback, track product performance, and make data-driven decisions to continuously improve your product offerings.

Expanding Your Product Catalog

As your brand grows, so too can your product catalog. We'll explore strategies for expanding your offerings, whether through new product development, partnerships, or collaborations. You'll learn how to stay innovative and keep your brand fresh in the eyes of your customers.

Key Takeaways

In this chapter, we've uncovered the critical aspects of crafting and selecting compelling products for your e-commerce brand. By understanding your audience, embracing sustainability, and employing effective product presentation, you'll be well-equipped to create a product catalog that resonates with your customers.

In Chapter 4, we'll shift our focus to the world of digital marketing, discussing the strategies and tactics to attract, engage, and retain customers in the competitive e-commerce landscape.

—-

This chapter serves as a comprehensive guide to help readers develop or curate products that align with their brand's vision and resonate with their target audience. It provides insights into the various facets of product development and selection while emphasizing the importance of sustainability and customer-centric approaches. Subsequent chapters will continue to build on this knowledge, helping readers navigate different aspects of e-commerce and brand-building.

4

Digital Marketing Strategies for E-commerce Success

Attracting, Engaging, and Retaining Customers in the Digital Age

In the previous chapters, we explored the foundation of your e-commerce business and how to create compelling products. Now, it's time to share those products with the world. Chapter 4 delves into the dynamic world of digital marketing, providing you with the strategies and tactics to attract, engage, and retain customers in the competitive e-commerce landscape.

The Digital Marketing Landscape

To succeed in e-commerce, you must navigate the ever-evolving digital marketing landscape. We'll explore the core components of digital marketing, including search engine optimization (SEO), search engine marketing (SEM), social media marketing, content marketing, email marketing, and influencer marketing. Understanding these channels is crucial for a well-rounded marketing strategy.

Crafting Your Brand's Digital Presence

Your brand's digital presence begins with a compelling website, but it extends to your presence on various platforms and channels. We'll discuss the importance of a cohesive and consistent brand identity across your website, social media, email campaigns, and advertising. A strong digital presence reinforces your brand's image and message.

Content Marketing and SEO

Content is king in the digital marketing world. We'll explore the power of content marketing in attracting and engaging your target audience. You'll learn how to create high-quality, relevant content that not only educates and entertains but also improves your search engine rankings through effective SEO techniques.

Paid Advertising and SEM

Paid advertising is a valuable tool to quickly reach potential customers. We'll discuss the intricacies of search engine marketing (SEM), display advertising, and pay-per-click (PPC) campaigns. You'll gain insights into budgeting, ad targeting, and the importance of continuous optimization to maximize your return on investment (ROI).

Social Media Marketing

Social media has become a cornerstone of digital marketing. We'll explore the key platforms, such as Facebook, Instagram, Twitter, and LinkedIn, and how to use them effectively to engage with your audience. You'll learn about content strategies, paid social advertising, and social media analytics.

Email Marketing

Email marketing remains a powerful tool for building and nurturing customer relationships. We'll discuss best practices for creating engaging email campaigns, building subscriber lists, and segmenting your audience for personalized communication. You'll also learn how to measure the effectiveness of your email marketing efforts.

Influencer Marketing

Influencer marketing leverages the reach and trust of influential individuals to promote your products. We'll explore the world of influencer partnerships, from identifying the right influencers for your brand to negotiating contracts and measuring the impact of influencer collaborations.

Retention Strategies

Acquiring new customers is essential, but retaining them is equally important. We'll delve into customer retention strategies, including loyalty programs, personalized recommendations, and exceptional customer service. A loyal customer base can become your brand's strongest advocates.

Analytics and Data-Driven Decision-Making

The success of your digital marketing efforts hinges on data. We'll discuss the importance of analytics and how to use data to measure the effectiveness of your marketing campaigns, identify areas for improvement, and make informed decisions to optimize your marketing strategy.

Key Takeaways

In this chapter, we've explored the multifaceted world of digital marketing. By understanding the various channels and tactics, you'll be better equipped to create a holistic marketing strategy that attracts, engages, and retains customers in the digital age.

In Chapter 5, we'll shift our focus to the customer experience, discussing how to create a seamless and enjoyable shopping journey that keeps your customers coming back for more.

—-

This chapter serves as a comprehensive guide to digital marketing in the context of e-commerce. It provides readers with a deep understanding of the various digital marketing channels and strategies to help them create effective campaigns that drive customer acquisition and retention. Subsequent chapters will continue to build on this knowledge, offering insights into other crucial aspects of e-commerce and brand-building.

5

Crafting a Seamless Customer Experience

elivering Exceptional Service from Browsing to Checkout

In the previous chapters, we've explored the foundations of e-commerce, product development, and digital marketing. Now, it's time to shift our focus to the heart of your brand: the customer experience. Chapter 5 delves into the strategies and practices for creating a seamless and enjoyable shopping journey that keeps your customers coming back for more.

The Importance of Customer Experience

The customer experience is more than just a buzzword; it's a fundamental aspect of e-commerce success. We'll discuss why a positive customer experience is critical, its impact on brand loyalty, and how it can differentiate your brand from the competition.

User-Centered Website Design

Your e-commerce website is the primary touchpoint with your customers.

We'll explore the principles of user-centered design, responsive web design, and the importance of mobile optimization. A user-friendly website not only enhances the customer experience but also contributes to higher conversion rates.

Navigational Simplicity

Navigation is a key element of the customer experience. We'll discuss the importance of intuitive website navigation, clear categorization, and effective search functionality. You'll learn how to ensure that customers can easily find what they're looking for, reducing frustration and improving satisfaction.

Seamless Checkout Process

The checkout process is the make-or-break point for many e-commerce transactions. We'll explore strategies for creating a seamless and secure checkout experience. This includes one-click checkout, multiple payment options, and transparent shipping costs. Reducing cart abandonment is key to improving conversion rates.

Personalization and Recommendations

Personalization can significantly enhance the customer experience. We'll discuss the use of customer data to provide personalized product recommendations, tailored content, and exclusive offers. Personalization not only boosts sales but also builds a stronger emotional connection with customers.

Exceptional Customer Service

Customer service is a cornerstone of the customer experience. We'll explore the elements of exceptional customer service, from responsive email support to live chat and social media interaction. You'll learn how to turn customer inquiries and issues into opportunities to build trust and loyalty.

Post-Purchase Engagement

The customer journey doesn't end at the checkout. We'll discuss post-purchase engagement strategies, such as order tracking, follow-up emails, and request for feedback. These practices not only keep customers informed but also create opportunities for cross-selling and repeat business.

Returns and Refunds

Returns and refunds are an inevitable part of e-commerce. We'll explore the importance of a clear and customer-friendly return policy. You'll learn how to handle returns efficiently and turn dissatisfied customers into loyal ones.

Measuring and Improving the Customer Experience

To continually enhance the customer experience, you need to measure and analyze your performance. We'll discuss the use of customer surveys, feedback forms, and website analytics to identify areas for improvement and make data-driven decisions.

Key Takeaways

In this chapter, we've delved into the world of customer experience. By focusing on user-centered design, navigation, seamless checkout, personalization, exceptional customer service, and post-purchase engagement, you'll be well-prepared to create a customer-centric e-commerce brand that keeps customers coming back for more.

In Chapter 6, we'll turn our attention to the global landscape of e-commerce, discussing how to expand your brand internationally and navigate the complexities of cross-border commerce.

—-

This chapter provides readers with a comprehensive understanding of the customer experience and its vital role in e-commerce success. It emphasizes the practical strategies and practices for delivering exceptional service at every stage of the customer journey. Subsequent chapters will continue to explore other crucial aspects of e-commerce and brand-building.

6

Expanding Globally: Navigating the World of International E-commerce

Taking Your Brand Across Borders

In the previous chapters, we've focused on the essentials of e-commerce, product development, digital marketing, and the customer experience. Now, it's time to think globally. Chapter 6 explores the dynamic world of international e-commerce, guiding you through the intricacies of taking your brand across borders.

The Global E-commerce Landscape

E-commerce knows no borders. We'll discuss the global e-commerce landscape, exploring the vast opportunities presented by international markets. You'll learn about the growing trend of cross-border shopping and why expanding globally is a strategic move for e-commerce brands.

Market Research and Selection

Before venturing into international markets, you must conduct comprehensive market research. We'll delve into the process of selecting the right markets based on factors such as market size, growth potential, cultural fit, and competition analysis. Your market selection is a critical first step in global expansion.

Localization and Cultural Sensitivity

Understanding and respecting the culture of your target markets is crucial. We'll discuss localization strategies, including language adaptation, cultural sensitivity, and the importance of tailoring your brand and content to resonate with local audiences.

Legal and Regulatory Considerations

Expanding internationally involves navigating a complex web of legal and regulatory requirements. We'll explore topics such as international trade regulations, taxes, customs, and data privacy. You'll learn how to ensure compliance with the laws of your target markets.

Payment and Currency Considerations

Payment methods and currency preferences vary from one country to another. We'll discuss the importance of offering diverse payment options, such as credit cards, digital wallets, and local payment methods. You'll also learn about currency conversion and the impact it can have on pricing.

Shipping and Logistics

Efficient shipping and logistics are essential for international e-commerce. We'll explore strategies for managing shipping costs, delivery times, and international fulfillment centers. You'll learn how to provide transparent and competitive shipping options to your global customers.

International Marketing and Customer Engagement

Your marketing strategy must adapt to the international landscape. We'll discuss the challenges and opportunities of international digital marketing, including multilingual SEO, localized content, and the use of cultural insights to engage international audiences.

Currency Exchange and Pricing Strategies

Fluctuating exchange rates can impact your pricing strategy. We'll explore currency exchange considerations and strategies for setting competitive prices in international markets. You'll learn how to manage currency risk and optimize your pricing strategy for global expansion.

Customer Support and Communication

Effective customer support extends to international markets. We'll discuss the importance of multilingual customer support, time zone considerations, and culturally sensitive communication. Providing a seamless experience for global customers is paramount.

Measuring International Success

To gauge your international success, you must measure performance and adapt accordingly. We'll discuss the use of analytics, customer feedback, and market-specific KPIs to evaluate your international e-commerce efforts and refine your strategy.

Key Takeaways

In this chapter, we've explored the world of international e-commerce. By understanding market selection, localization, legal considerations, payment and currency strategies, and international marketing, you'll be well-prepared to take your brand across borders and tap into the global e-commerce opportunity.

In Chapter 7, we'll explore the role of technology and innovation in e-commerce, discussing the latest trends and how to stay at the forefront of the industry.

—-

This chapter provides readers with a comprehensive understanding of the complexities and opportunities in international e-commerce. It emphasizes the importance of market research, localization, and compliance, while offering practical insights into the various aspects of expanding a brand globally. Subsequent chapters will continue to explore other crucial aspects of e-commerce and brand-building.

7

Technology and Innovation in E-commerce

Staying Ahead in the Digital Revolution

In the previous chapters, we've explored the essential components of e-commerce, from foundational principles to global expansion. Now, it's time to discuss the driving force behind e-commerce evolution: technology and innovation. Chapter 7 delves into the latest trends, emerging technologies, and strategies to stay at the forefront of the e-commerce industry.

The Rapid Pace of Technological Change

E-commerce is a dynamic and ever-changing field. We'll discuss the rapid pace of technological advancements and how staying informed about emerging trends is essential for e-commerce brands. Adapting to new technologies can provide a competitive edge.

Mobile Commerce and Responsive Design

Mobile commerce is on the rise. We'll explore the importance of mobile optimization, responsive design, and the use of mobile apps to cater to the growing number of customers who prefer shopping on their smartphones and tablets.

Artificial Intelligence (AI) and Machine Learning

AI and machine learning have transformative potential in e-commerce. We'll discuss the applications of AI in customer recommendations, chatbots, and personalization. You'll learn how to harness AI to enhance customer experiences and streamline operations.

Augmented Reality (AR) and Virtual Reality (VR)

AR and VR technologies are changing the way customers shop online. We'll explore how these technologies enable immersive experiences, such as virtual try-ons for fashion and interactive product visualizations. You'll learn how to leverage AR and VR to engage customers and boost sales.

Voice Commerce and Smart Assistants

Voice-activated devices and smart assistants are becoming increasingly popular. We'll discuss voice commerce and how e-commerce brands can adapt to this trend. You'll learn how to optimize your content and marketing for voice search.

Blockchain and Cryptocurrency

Blockchain technology has the potential to revolutionize online transactions. We'll explore the applications of blockchain in e-commerce, including supply chain transparency, secure payments, and customer trust. You'll gain insights into the role of cryptocurrency in the e-commerce landscape.

Sustainable E-commerce

Sustainability is a growing concern for consumers. We'll discuss the importance of sustainability in e-commerce, from eco-friendly packaging to carbon offset programs. You'll learn how to incorporate sustainable practices into your brand's ethos.

Data Security and Privacy

Data security and privacy are paramount. We'll explore the latest in data protection regulations and best practices for safeguarding customer information. You'll learn how to build trust by prioritizing data security.

Automation and Efficiency

Automation can streamline e-commerce operations. We'll discuss the use of automation in inventory management, order processing, and customer support. You'll discover how to free up resources and improve efficiency through smart automation.

Continuous Learning and Adaptation

Staying at the forefront of e-commerce requires a commitment to continuous learning. We'll discuss the importance of staying informed about industry trends, attending conferences, and networking. You'll gain insights into how to foster a culture of innovation within your brand.

Key Takeaways

In this chapter, we've explored the role of technology and innovation in e-commerce. By understanding the latest trends and emerging technologies, you'll be well-prepared to embrace innovation and stay ahead in the digital revolution.

In Chapter 8, we'll delve into the art of measuring success and adapting to change. We'll discuss how to set and track key performance indicators (KPIs) and implement strategies for growth and resilience.

—-

This chapter provides readers with a comprehensive understanding of the role of technology and innovation in e-commerce. It emphasizes the importance of staying up-to-date with the latest trends and emerging technologies to remain competitive in the ever-evolving e-commerce landscape. Subsequent chapters will continue to explore other crucial aspects of e-commerce and brand-building.

8

Measuring Success and Adapting to Change

S etting and Tracking KPIs for E-commerce Growth

In the previous chapters, we've explored various facets of e-commerce, from foundational principles to technological innovation. Now, it's time to discuss how to measure success and adapt to change. Chapter 8 delves into the art of setting and tracking key performance indicators (KPIs) to ensure the growth and resilience of your e-commerce brand.

The Importance of Measuring Success

Measuring success is not just about celebrating victories; it's about continuous improvement. We'll discuss the importance of defining success for your e-commerce brand and how KPIs are the yardsticks of achievement.

Setting Meaningful KPIs

Effective KPIs are specific, measurable, achievable, relevant, and time-bound

(SMART). We'll explore how to set meaningful KPIs that align with your business objectives. Whether it's increasing sales, improving customer retention, or expanding into new markets, your KPIs should reflect your brand's goals.

Financial KPIs

Financial KPIs are critical for e-commerce brands. We'll discuss KPIs such as revenue, profit margins, and customer lifetime value. You'll learn how to measure financial performance and use these metrics to guide decision-making.

Customer-Centric KPIs

Your customers are at the core of your success. We'll explore KPIs related to customer satisfaction, retention, and acquisition. You'll gain insights into how to measure and improve the customer experience.

Marketing and Conversion KPIs

Marketing is a significant driver of e-commerce success. We'll discuss KPIs related to digital marketing, such as conversion rates, click-through rates, and customer acquisition cost. You'll learn how to track the performance of your marketing efforts and optimize your strategies.

Operational and Efficiency KPIs

Operational efficiency is essential for sustainability. We'll explore KPIs related to order fulfillment, inventory turnover, and shipping times. You'll discover how to identify bottlenecks and streamline your operations.

Data Analytics and Business Intelligence

Effective measurement requires data analytics and business intelligence tools. We'll discuss the use of analytics platforms and dashboards to gather, analyze, and visualize data. You'll learn how to make data-driven decisions based on insights derived from KPI tracking.

Adaptation and Resilience

E-commerce is a dynamic field, and adaptability is key to long-term success. We'll explore the importance of resilience and how to adapt to changes in the industry, market conditions, and customer preferences. You'll gain insights into strategies for staying ahead of the curve.

Continuous Improvement

Measuring success is not a one-time effort; it's an ongoing process. We'll discuss the importance of continuous improvement and how to use KPIs to identify areas for growth and optimization. You'll learn how to foster a culture of learning and adaptability within your brand.

Case Studies

Throughout this chapter, we'll present real-world case studies of e-commerce brands that have successfully used KPIs to measure and achieve their goals. These examples will provide practical insights and inspiration for your own e-commerce journey.

Key Takeaways

In this chapter, we've explored the art of setting and tracking KPIs for e-commerce success. By understanding the importance of measurement, setting meaningful KPIs, and using data analytics, you'll be well-prepared to measure and adapt to change, fostering the growth and resilience of your brand.

In Chapter 10, we'll take a deep dive into the art of sustainability in e-commerce. We'll discuss the importance of eco-friendly practices, corporate social responsibility, and the role of sustainability in building a 21st-century brand.

—-

This chapter provides readers with a comprehensive understanding of the importance of measuring success and adapting to change in the context of e-commerce. It emphasizes the role of KPIs and data analytics in guiding decision-making and continuous improvement. Subsequent chapters will continue to explore other crucial aspects of e-commerce and brand-building.

9

Sustainability in E-commerce

Embracing Eco-Friendly Practices and Social Responsibility

In the previous chapters, we've covered various aspects of e-commerce, from foundational principles to measuring success. Now, it's time to discuss the critical role of sustainability in e-commerce. Chapter 10 delves into the importance of eco-friendly practices, corporate social responsibility, and the role of sustainability in building a 21st-century brand.

The Sustainable E-commerce Revolution

Sustainability is no longer an optional consideration; it's a global imperative. We'll discuss how sustainability is revolutionizing the e-commerce industry, from packaging to product sourcing. Consumers are increasingly drawn to eco-conscious brands, making sustainability a strategic advantage.

Sustainable Packaging and Shipping

The environmental impact of packaging and shipping cannot be ignored. We'll explore strategies for adopting sustainable packaging materials, reducing waste, and optimizing shipping routes to minimize carbon emissions. You'll learn how to balance customer expectations with eco-friendly practices.

Sustainable Product Sourcing

The products you sell have a significant impact on sustainability. We'll discuss the importance of ethical and sustainable product sourcing, including fair trade practices, eco-friendly materials, and responsible manufacturing. You'll learn how to make environmentally conscious choices without compromising quality.

Carbon Footprint Reduction

Reducing your brand's carbon footprint is a critical sustainability goal. We'll explore strategies for measuring and reducing your carbon emissions, from optimizing logistics to investing in renewable energy. You'll discover how to align your brand with carbon neutrality and climate action.

Corporate Social Responsibility (CSR)

Corporate social responsibility is an integral part of a 21st-century brand. We'll discuss the importance of giving back to society, supporting local communities, and aligning your brand with causes that resonate with your values. CSR not only benefits society but also enhances your brand's reputation.

Transparency and Accountability

Transparency is key to building trust with environmentally conscious consumers. We'll explore the importance of transparent communication about your sustainability efforts. You'll learn how to provide visibility into your sourcing practices, production processes, and the environmental impact of your products.

Communicating Sustainability to Customers

Effectively communicating your sustainability efforts is a crucial step. We'll discuss strategies for educating customers about your eco-friendly practices, whether through your website, marketing materials, or product labels. You'll learn how to engage and inspire your audience with your commitment to sustainability.

Eco-Friendly Partnerships and Collaborations

Collaborations with like-minded organizations can amplify your sustainability efforts. We'll explore the benefits of eco-friendly partnerships, from co-branded products to joint sustainability initiatives. You'll gain insights into how collaborations can expand your brand's impact.

Case Studies

Throughout this chapter, we'll present real-world case studies of e-commerce brands that have successfully integrated sustainability into their business model. These examples will provide practical insights and inspiration for your own sustainability journey.

Key Takeaways

In this chapter, we've explored the importance of sustainability in e-commerce. By understanding the role of eco-friendly packaging, sustainable product sourcing, carbon footprint reduction, corporate social responsibility, transparency, and effective communication, you'll be well-prepared to embrace sustainability as a cornerstone of your brand in the 21st century.

In Chapter 11, we'll discuss the future of e-commerce and explore the trends, challenges, and opportunities that lie ahead for brands in the digital age.

—-

This chapter provides readers with a comprehensive understanding of the importance of sustainability in e-commerce and how to incorporate eco-friendly practices and social responsibility into their brand's ethos. It emphasizes the significance of sustainability as a strategic advantage in the modern e-commerce landscape. Subsequent chapters will continue to explore other crucial aspects of e-commerce and brand-building.

10

The Future of E-commerce

Navigating Trends, Challenges, and Opportunities in the Digital Age

In the previous chapters, we've explored various aspects of e-commerce, from foundational principles to sustainability. Now, it's time to turn our attention to the future of e-commerce. Chapter 10 delves into the trends, challenges, and opportunities that lie ahead for brands in the digital age.

The Ever-Evolving E-commerce Landscape

E-commerce is in a constant state of flux. We'll discuss how staying informed about the latest industry trends and technological advancements is crucial for e-commerce brands looking to remain competitive and relevant.

E-commerce Trends

We'll explore the most prominent trends shaping the e-commerce landscape, from the rise of mobile shopping to the increasing importance of social commerce and the impact of AI and machine learning on customer experiences. Staying ahead of these trends can position your brand for success.

Challenges in E-commerce

Challenges are part of the e-commerce journey. We'll discuss common challenges, such as increased competition, data privacy regulations, and cybersecurity threats. You'll learn how to anticipate and address these obstacles to maintain business continuity.

Opportunities on the Horizon

Amid challenges, opportunities arise. We'll delve into emerging opportunities in e-commerce, including global expansion into untapped markets, the potential for AR and VR integration, and the growth of the subscription and direct-to-consumer (DTC) models. Identifying and capitalizing on these opportunities can drive your brand's growth.

Sustainability as a Competitive Advantage

Sustainability is more than a trend; it's a competitive advantage. We'll discuss the long-term benefits of eco-friendly practices, corporate social responsibility, and transparency. You'll learn how sustainability can set your brand apart and attract environmentally conscious consumers.

Innovation and Adaptation

In a rapidly changing landscape, innovation and adaptation are essential. We'll explore how fostering a culture of innovation and adaptability within your brand can ensure long-term success. Staying ahead of the curve requires a commitment to continuous learning and improvement.

Preparing for the Future

To thrive in the future of e-commerce, preparation is key. We'll discuss how to create a roadmap for your brand's growth, setting short-term and long-term goals, and ensuring your team is equipped with the skills and knowledge needed to navigate the ever-evolving e-commerce landscape.

Case Studies

Throughout this chapter, we'll present real-world case studies of e-commerce brands that have effectively embraced industry trends, tackled challenges, and capitalized on emerging opportunities. These examples will provide practical insights and inspiration for your own e-commerce journey.

Key Takeaways

In this chapter, we've explored the future of e-commerce. By understanding the latest trends, challenges, and opportunities, you'll be well-prepared to navigate the evolving digital age and position your brand for long-term success.

In the final chapter, Chapter 10, we'll summarize the key takeaways from the entire book and offer a closing message to inspire and empower readers in their e-commerce endeavors.

—-

This chapter provides readers with a comprehensive understanding of the future of e-commerce, offering insights into the trends, challenges, and opportunities that will shape the industry. It emphasizes the importance of preparation, innovation, and adaptability in the face of constant change. Subsequent chapters will continue to explore other crucial aspects of e-commerce and brand-building.

11

Embracing the Future

Summarizing Key Takeaways and Inspiring Your E-commerce Journey

In the previous chapters, we've embarked on a comprehensive journey through the world of e-commerce, covering essential principles, product development, digital marketing, the customer experience, international expansion, technology and innovation, sustainability, and the future of the industry. In this final chapter, we'll summarize the key takeaways from the entire book and offer a closing message to inspire and empower you in your e-commerce endeavors.

Reflecting on Your E-commerce Journey

Your journey through this book has been an exploration of the e-commerce ecosystem. We've covered numerous aspects, from building a strong foundation to staying ahead of the latest industry trends. Take a moment to reflect on the knowledge and insights you've gained.

Key Takeaways

Let's revisit the key takeaways from each chapter:

- Chapter 1: Establish a clear brand identity that resonates with your target audience.
  - Chapter 2: Build a solid foundation for your e-commerce business with effective planning and strategy.
  - Chapter 3: Craft compelling products tailored to your audience's needs and preferences.
  - Chapter 4: Embrace digital marketing strategies to attract, engage, and retain customers.
  - Chapter 5: Prioritize the customer experience, from website design to post-purchase engagement.
  - Chapter 6: Explore international expansion and navigate the complexities of cross-border e-commerce.
  - Chapter 7: Embrace technological innovation to stay competitive in the digital age.
  - Chapter 8: Measure success and adapt to change through the use of key performance indicators (KPIs).
  - Chapter 9: Embrace sustainability and corporate social responsibility to differentiate your brand.
  - Chapter 10: Anticipate and capitalize on the future trends, challenges, and opportunities in e-commerce.

Your E-commerce Roadmap

As you navigate the world of e-commerce, keep your journey in mind:

1. Know Your Brand: Establish a clear brand identity and purpose.
2. Plan Wisely: Build a solid foundation for your e-commerce business.
3. Create Compelling Products: Craft products that meet your audience's needs.
4. Market Strategically: Embrace digital marketing to attract, engage, and

retain customers.

5. Prioritize the Customer: Enhance the customer experience at every touchpoint.
6. Expand Globally: Navigate international expansion with strategy and sensitivity.
7. Embrace Innovation: Stay at the forefront of technological trends.
8. Measure Success: Set and track KPIs to guide your decisions.
9. Prioritize Sustainability: Differentiate your brand with eco-friendly practices and social responsibility.
10. Embrace the Future: Anticipate industry changes and adapt to opportunities.

Your E-commerce Legacy

Your e-commerce journey is a continuous evolution. As you move forward, keep these key messages in mind:

- Embrace Change: The e-commerce landscape is ever-evolving. Embrace change and innovation as opportunities for growth.

- Prioritize Sustainability: Sustainability isn't just a trend; it's a strategic advantage. Eco-friendly practices and social responsibility can set your brand apart.

- Stay Informed: Continuously educate yourself about industry trends, emerging technologies, and customer behaviors.

- Foster Innovation: Foster a culture of innovation and adaptability within your brand to remain competitive.

- Measure and Adapt: Use KPIs to measure success and adapt to change for continuous improvement.

- Create Value: Always seek to create value for your customers and society, not just revenue.

- Connect with Purpose: Building a 21st-century brand means connecting with purpose, both internally and externally.

Closing Message

Your journey in e-commerce is an exciting and ever-evolving adventure. Whether you're just starting or have been in the industry for years, remember that success in e-commerce is built on a foundation of continuous learning, innovation, adaptability, and a commitment to creating value for your customers and the world.

Thank you for joining us on this journey through "E-commerce Evolution: Building a 21st Century Brand." As you embrace the future, may your e-commerce endeavors be marked by growth, resilience, and positive impact.

Good luck, and here's to a successful and fulfilling e-commerce journey!

12

Resources and Tools for E-commerce Success

Comprehensive Guide to E-commerce Tools and Platforms

In the previous chapters, we've explored the diverse aspects of e-commerce, from building a brand identity to embracing the future of the industry. Now, it's time to provide you with a comprehensive guide to the resources and tools that can facilitate your e-commerce success.

The E-commerce Toolkit

Just as a craftsman needs the right tools, an e-commerce entrepreneur requires a set of resources to thrive in the digital marketplace. This chapter will serve as your toolkit, offering insights and recommendations for a wide range of tools, platforms, and resources.

Website and E-commerce Platforms

The foundation of your online business is your website. We'll explore popular website and e-commerce platforms, including Shopify, WooCommerce, BigCommerce, Magento, and more. You'll learn which platform aligns with your business needs and budget.

Payment Processors

Efficient and secure payment processing is vital. We'll discuss popular payment processors like PayPal, Stripe, and Square. You'll gain insights into their features, transaction fees, and suitability for different business models.

Shipping and Fulfillment Tools

Shipping and order fulfillment are critical components of e-commerce. We'll delve into shipping solutions such as ShipStation, Easyship, and Shippo. You'll learn how these tools can streamline your logistics.

Digital Marketing and SEO Tools

Digital marketing is a cornerstone of e-commerce success. We'll explore tools for SEO, social media management, email marketing, and paid advertising, including Google Analytics, SEMrush, Mailchimp, Hootsuite, and more. You'll discover how these tools can enhance your marketing efforts.

Customer Relationship Management (CRM) Software

Maintaining strong customer relationships is essential. We'll discuss CRM software like HubSpot, Salesforce, and Zoho CRM. You'll learn how these platforms can help you manage and nurture customer connections.

Analytics and Data Insights

Data-driven decision-making is a powerful tool. We'll explore analytics tools such as Google Analytics, Hotjar, and Kissmetrics. You'll discover how these platforms provide insights to measure and improve your performance.

Design and Creativity Tools

Visually appealing content is crucial in e-commerce. We'll discuss design and creativity tools, including Adobe Creative Cloud, Canva, and Pixlr. You'll gain insights into creating eye-catching visuals for your brand.

Inventory and Order Management

Efficient inventory and order management are essential for smooth operations. We'll explore tools like TradeGecko, Skubana, and Ordoro. You'll learn how these platforms help you stay organized.

Marketing Automation

Automation can save time and boost productivity. We'll discuss marketing automation tools, including HubSpot, Marketo, and Pardot. You'll gain insights into automating marketing campaigns and customer interactions.

Security and Data Protection

Data security is paramount. We'll explore security and data protection tools, such as Sucuri, Norton, and LastPass. You'll learn how to safeguard your e-commerce business from cyber threats.

Case Studies

Throughout this chapter, we'll present real-world case studies of e-commerce brands that have effectively leveraged various tools and resources to streamline their operations, enhance their marketing efforts, and improve their customer experiences.

Key Takeaways

In this chapter, we've provided you with a comprehensive guide to resources and tools for e-commerce success. By understanding the tools and platforms available to you, you'll be well-equipped to build and grow your e-commerce business efficiently and effectively.

With this toolkit, you have the resources you need to take your e-commerce brand to the next level. May these tools serve as valuable assets on your journey to building a successful 21st-century e-commerce brand.

Thank you for joining us in this comprehensive exploration of e-commerce, and we wish you the utmost success in your e-commerce endeavors.

—-

This chapter serves as a valuable resource for readers, providing them with a comprehensive guide to various tools and platforms that can facilitate their e-commerce success. It emphasizes the importance of choosing the right tools to streamline operations, enhance marketing efforts, and improve customer experiences. This resource-rich chapter concludes the book and equips readers with the tools they need to thrive in the world of e-commerce.

"E-commerce Evolution: Building a 21st Century Brand" is a comprehensive book that explores the various facets of e-commerce and brand-building. The book is divided into twelve chapters, each addressing a crucial aspect of creating and growing a successful e-commerce business.

Chapter 1: The book begins with the importance of establishing a clear brand identity that resonates with the target audience.

Chapter 2: It then delves into building a strong foundation for the e-commerce business, emphasizing effective planning and strategy.

Chapter 3: Crafting compelling products tailored to the audience's needs and preferences is discussed in the third chapter.

Chapter 4: The role of digital marketing strategies in attracting, engaging, and retaining customers is explored in the next chapter.

Chapter 5: Prioritizing the customer experience, from website design to post-purchase engagement, is the focus of the fifth chapter.

Chapter 6: International expansion and the complexities of cross-border e-commerce are discussed, highlighting the strategies for global growth.

Chapter 7: The importance of technology and innovation in staying competitive in the digital age is the central theme of this chapter.

Chapter 8: The book delves into the art of measuring success and adapting to change, emphasizing the use of key performance indicators (KPIs).

Chapter 9: Sustainability and corporate social responsibility are highlighted as crucial differentiators in building a 21st-century brand.

Chapter 10: The final chapters offer insights into the future of e-commerce, including trends, challenges, and opportunities.

Chapter 11: The book concludes with a toolkit, summarizing a wide range of tools, platforms, and resources for e-commerce success.

Each chapter provides valuable insights, case studies, and practical recommendations for readers looking to build and grow their e-commerce brand. The book underscores the importance of innovation, adaptability, sustainability, and continuous learning in the dynamic e-commerce landscape. Readers are equipped with the knowledge and resources to create a thriving 21st-century e-commerce brand.